Voyager
Passport D

Fluency 1

MW00679526

ISBN 978-1-4168-0466-6

Copyright 2008 by Voyager Expanded Learning, L.P.

All rights reserved. No part of this publication may be reproduced or transmitted in any form or by any means, electronic or mechanical, including photocopy, recording, or any information storage and retrieval system, without permission in writing from the publisher.

Printed in the United States of America

07 08 09 10 11 12 13   PAD   9 8 7 6 5 4 3 2 1

Table of Contents

Fluency Practice

 Read the story to each other.

 Read the story on your own.

 Read the story to your partner again. Try to read the story even better.

 Questions? Ask your partner two questions about the story. Tell each other about the story you just read.

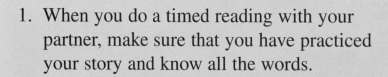

Timed Reading

1. When you do a timed reading with your partner, make sure that you have practiced your story and know all the words.

2. When you are ready, tell your partner to start the timer.

3. Read carefully, and your partner will stop you at 1 minute. When you stop, mark your place.

4. Count the total number of words you read.

5. In the back of your Student Book, write the number of words you read and color in the squares on your Fluency Chart.

6. Now switch with your partner.

Twirling

The girl was the first in line at the shop. She had saved for months and had her cash in her purse. She wanted a baton so she could learn to twirl and lead the band. She asked the clerk for the baton.

He turned and said, "We are out." The girl was on the verge of tears.

Then a man came in with a box. "I have a return," he said.

The clerk opened the box, and there was a baton. The girl got the baton and learned to twirl and whirl it. Now she leads the band! ⑨⑨

Baseball

Baseball is a fun game to play. It has many rules to learn. Here are a few facts about it.

- It is played with a bat and ball by two teams of nine players on a field.
- Each team takes turns in the field and at bat.
- The team batting tries to hit the ball so that they can run all the bases and score.
- The team with the most runs at the end of the game wins.

Would you like to know more? There are many good books about baseball in the library. Go have a look! ⑨⑧

Ice-Skating

Sam watched Trish glide over the ice. She jumped and twirled without slipping. Sam wished he could skate. Trish skated up and sat for a quick rest. "Come skate, Sam," she said.

"I do not know how," he told her.

Trish said she would teach Sam. He pulled on skates and laced them up. The two stepped out on the ice. Sam took a step and fell. But he got up. He hung onto Trish and took more steps. She helped him, and he crossed the ice. He went faster. He was skating!

Now Sam and Trish skate each day.⑽⓪

Joan and Nan

Joan lived on a farm with her pet goat Nan. Each day she fed Nan toast and oats and brushed her coat. Then they would walk up the road.

One day they went out to roam and walked all the way to the tall bridge by the ridge. They started across when Nan came to a halt. "Come on," said Joan, but the goat would not budge because she was scared. They had to get home!

Then Joan felt something in her coat. She had a bit of fudge. With one whiff, the goat turned and walked home with Joan! ⓸⓿⓿

Farms

There are many different kinds of farms. Some are small, and some are large.

Some grow crops such as hay, grain, soy beans, oats, greens, or corn. Crops are planted in the soil and grow. They are used for food.

Some farms raise animals. In the barn or yard, you may find goats, sheep, pigs, chicks, or cows. Animal farms may get paid for eggs, milk, or cheese or even goat or sheep hair to make wool.

Other farms grow the fruit that we eat such as plums, grapes, or pears. What kind of farm would you like to see?(100)

Phil and the Farm

Phil spent each June with Gramps on the farm. He helped round up the animals with the old hound dog and worked on the grounds. But what he liked best was fishing with Gramps. For years he went to the brook to try to catch the big trout, but it always found a way off the hook. Still, it was fun, so off they went.

He sat on the ground and tossed out his line. As he was looking up at the clouds, he felt a tug. He had hooked the big trout! Gramps was so proud he took a photo.⑩⑴

A Gift

What would you do if you owned part of a beach? Joe Brown gave his beach away. Joe's family had a house on the beach for many years. But strong winds and heavy rain had hurt the house. Joe had to decide what to do. ㊺

Joe thought about fixing the house. He thought about selling the land. After all, he could make more than $2 million. But Joe gave the land to the city. Now it is a place where everyone can go. Everyone can enjoy the beauty of the beach.

Thanking the Heroes

All towns have heroes. Think about the people who work hard to keep you safe, happy, and healthy. They solve problems in your town every day.

One town solved a problem on its own. The people wanted to find a way to thank their heroes.㊺ The town wanted to thank the police, the firefighters, the teachers, and other heroes in the town.

The people in the town all got together. They cooked a big lunch for their heroes. The children made gifts for them. It was a great way to say, "Thank you."

Help at the Library

"Remember your homework," said Mr. Boyd. "Make a paper airplane. Bring it to school. We will have a race to see which one flies the farthest."

Elise went home. She tried four ways to make an airplane. None of them flew far at all. Elise felt sad.

"Let's go to the library," Dad said. "Mrs. Williams can help."⑤⑧

Elise did not know how the librarian could help. When they got there, she understood. Mrs. Williams knew all about the books in the library. She helped Elise find a book. It was about how to make paper airplanes. Elise thanked Mrs. Williams, and she and her dad went home. She couldn't wait to find the best one.

Caring for the Wild Animals

Do you know what to do if you find a hurt squirrel or a baby bird? Leave it alone. Call someone who knows how to care for wild animals.

Julie works at the Big Sky Wildcare Center. She takes care of birds that are sick or hurt. She helps them get healthy again. She makes sure they stay wild. Then she helps them get back to where they belong.⑥⑨

A lot of wild animals get hurt. The best way to help them is to find a group like Julie's. They know a lot about wild animals like owls, deer, and squirrels. They will come look at the animal you find. They might take it to an animal doctor. They will work hard to make sure the animal gets back to its home soon.

A Gentle Gorilla

It was a warm summer day in 1996. Many people were visiting the zoo. One of them was a 3-year-old boy. The group he was with went to see the gorillas.

The boy was excited. He climbed on the rail to get a good look at the gorillas. He slipped and fell down into the gorillas' home. What would happen?

People tried to get to the boy. A gorilla named Binti Jua got to him first. "What will she do?" people wondered. They were afraid the big gorilla would hurt the little boy. ⑨⑤

Binti Jua didn't hurt the boy. She picked him up gently. She took the boy to a door. It was the door the zoo workers used.

Some say Binti Jua took the boy there because she knew the boy was a person. She knew a zoo worker would come to the door. She knew a person could take care of the boy.

A zoo worker did take the boy from the door. Binti Jua had saved him. The boy went to a hospital, and now he is fine.

Kate's Hero

Jeff turned off the TV. He thought about the story he had just seen on the news. He got a big sheet of paper and a marker. This is what he wrote. (32)

Baby Kate is sick.
We are having a yard sale to raise money to help her.
Look for things at home that you want to sell.
Bring them to the library on Saturday.
We will be there from 9 a.m. to 5 p.m. (75)

Jeff's mom made copies of his sign. They put signs up all over town. The next Saturday, they had the yard sale. (97)

Jeff raised more than $1,000. He gave the money to Kate's family. They used it to pay the doctors who helped Kate. When Kate was 2 years old, she met Jeff. He is her hero.

Meet Alice Reed

The children in town had too much time on their hands. At least that is what the grown-ups said. "These kids need something to do after school," said Mrs. Hubert.

"I know," said Mrs. Tomball. "They seem to get into trouble every day. Have you seen the mess they made at the park?"

"I saw it," said Mr. Smith. "They left trash everywhere."

No one knew what to do. They just knew they did not like what the kids were doing after school. That is when Alice Reed spoke up. "I know what to do," she said.⑱

Alice was a painter. She painted beautiful pictures. She let all the kids in town know that she was giving free art classes every day after school.

The next week Alice's house was full of kids. Every day after school, the kids came to learn how to paint. After a few weeks, they had learned a lot. They had painted many good pictures. "Thank you, Alice," everyone said.

Painting It Right

Alice Reed's after-school art classes were great. The people in the town were happy that she was helping the children. The kids were happy that they were learning to paint.

One day Alice had another good idea. "What do you think we could do for our town?" she asked the kids. No one answered. "Have you seen spray paint on some of the walls downtown?" The kids nodded.

"We could try to clean it," someone said. ⑦⑦

"I think you're right," Alice said.

Alice helped the kids think of a plan. They held an art sale. They sold their paintings. Then they used the money to buy paint. They painted over the words on the buildings. The walls looked clean and new again.

The kids also painted a beautiful picture on a fence at the park. Everyone in town talked about the good things the kids had done. Alice Reed had made things better.

Word List

but	chance
each	face
could	football
planning	know
bridge	of
one	write